T0198895

DONNIE'S FIRST NIGHTMARE

Written by

Donna T. Thomas

AuthorHouse™
1663 Liberty Drive
Bloomington, IN 47403
www.authorhouse.com
Phone: 1 (800) 839-8640

Because of the dynamic nature of the Internet, any web addresses or links contained in this book may have changed since publication and may no longer be valid. The views expressed in this work are solely those of the author and do not necessarily reflect the views of the publisher, and the publisher hereby disclaims any responsibility for them.

Any people depicted in stock imagery provided by Getty Images are models, and such images are being used for illustrative purposes only.
Certain stock imagery © Getty Images.

This book is printed on acid-free paper.

ISBN: 978-1-7283-6063-8 (sc)
978-1-7283-6062-1 (e)

Library of Congress Control Number: 2020907855

Print information available on the last page.

Published by AuthorHouse 05/04/2020

authorHOUSE®

To my one and only Adonnis,
Mommy loves you always

One night Mama tuck Donnie into bed, No nightmare's, No nightmare's, I hope she said.

As Donnie closed his eyes and fell fast asleep Mama whispered night, night. He could hear loud noises coming from the window.

Oh noooooo! Oh noooooo!

He could hear the fire trucks going by and the horns of the cars that go beep, beep through the night.

People yelling, dogs barking woof, woof and music playing.

Donnie woke up in fear his little ears could not take the sound.

Soooo Donnie put his hands over his ears. Then he began to clap his hands, clap! clap! hoping it would go away.

He shook his head and put the pillow over his face.

Donnie woke up scared very late at night. It was so dark Donnie could not see his hands so he could count 1,2,3,4,5. Counting keeps him calm.

He was already having a hard time sleeping.

Oh dear! Oh dear! Mama forgot his night light.

He dash down the hallway with tears in his eyes. Running to Mama in the dark with no light.

Through the door he runs, whoosh, whoosh saying Mama! Mama! down the long hallway in a loud voice!

Mama wakes up and says what's wrong? Donnie is shaking and trying to pull Mama close.

Mama said it's alright, You can sleep with me tonight.

As he jumped in the bed Mama gives him a kiss and say's shhh night, night time for bed.

I love you she whispered while rubbing his head. Donnie stopped shaking. The noise that he heard before went away.

Mama started singing the ABC song to him, as he fell fast asleep hugging Mama oh so gently.

THe ENd

Printed in the United States
By Bookmasters